THE
LONE HARANGUER
RIDES AGAIN

Brant Parker and Johnny Hart

FAWCETT GOLD MEDAL • NEW YORK

A Fawcett Gold Medal Book

Published by Ballantine Books

ISBN 0-449-12688-9

This edition published by arrangement with Field Enterprises, Inc.

Manufactured in the United States of America

First Fawcett Gold Medal Edition: October 1982
First Ballantine Books Edition: November 1983

6-13

6-18

GALOOP
GALOOP
GALOOP
GALOOP
GALOOP
GALOOP
GALOOP
GALOOP
GALOOP

SWISH

THE KING IS A FINK

2-27

3-4

3-10

3-15

3-27

4-18

4·22

5-8

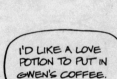

5-15

6.23

6-28

7·2

7-7

7-9

7-10

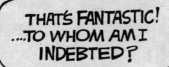

7-15

7-16

7-21

7-23

7-24

THE CUCKOO IS BROKE

HE HAS TO MAKE HIS PAYMENTS JUST THE SAME

8-26

8-30